P9-DFP-116

I NEED TO STOP DRINKING!

LIZ HEMINGWAY

~Freedom Publishing~

Copyright © 2013 Liz Hemingway
I Need To Stop Drinking!
Freedom Publishing

All rights reserved. No part of this publication may be reproduced, distributed, or transmitted in any form or by any means, including photocopying, recording, or other electronic or mechanical methods, without the prior written permission of the publisher, except in the case of brief quotations embodied in critical reviews and certain other non-commercial uses permitted by copyright law.

Times New Roman and Bradley Hand fonts used with permission from Microsoft.

DISCLAIMER

All advice given in this book has been written in good faith. However, the advice should be acted upon entirely at your own risk. The author accepts no responsibility. If you have been drinking alcohol daily or in very large amounts, then you should attempt to stop drinking only under strict medical supervision.

Only my close family and friends know that I drank far too much. But no-one in the whole world knows how many mornings I have woken up after a night's drinking, crying with the pain of it all. I cried at having done this to myself yet again and wondered if I would ever get free.

Liz Hemingway

For my long-suffering husband who has loved me and worried about me. The one who has put up with my drunken ways and was always able to see the best in me, even when I was at my very worst.

Thank you!

CONTENTS

INTRODUCTION

I need to stop drinking! Have you ever had any of these thoughts?

> ➢ I need to stop drinking because I am ruining my life!

> ➢ I need to stop drinking because I am wasting my money!

> ➢ I need to stop drinking because I am fed up with these horrible hangovers!

How many times have you said the immortal words "Never again," only to do exactly the same thing that night or a few days later? You ask yourself why you keep on hurting yourself like this. You need to escape this destructive path that you have found yourself on, but alcohol keeps calling you back, time and time again.

You continue to find plenty of reasons why you don't want to stop drinking. Do any of these reasons sound familiar to you?

> Drinking is my only pleasure in life, and it makes me happy!
> Drinking helps me get through the day or the evening.
> Drinking makes me happy.
> Alcohol relieves my stress and boredom.
> Drinking makes me forget my worries.
> All my friends drink, so I will end up isolated from them if I stop.
> I can control my drinking and can stop anytime.
> Alcohol is my only form of entertainment.
> I deserve a drink.
> What will I do with myself if I stop drinking?
> How will I explain to people that I have given up?
> It is too difficult to give up.

The list goes on and on.

It all seems so hopeless! You can't live with alcohol, and you can't live without it. Right?

Wrong!

I have amazing news for you that you will probably find difficult to believe at the moment. But please open your heart and mind up to the possibility of the truth of the next few sentences. Do not just skim over them, but truly consider the real possibilities that lie ahead for you if you stop drinking.

You can live a happy, joyful, and peaceful life without alcohol!

It is possible.

You can have more fun **without** drinking, and you can get rid of the pain and hurt that alcohol brings you.

You can live a better life and breathe a sigh of relief that you have escaped from its clutches.

I am living proof that this is possible. I have struggled with alcohol - boy have I struggled - but I have won the battle, and I am so grateful! My life has never been better, and your life can be better too. Much better! This is my story.

THE ROUGH HISTORY OF A PROBLEM DRINKER

> *"First the man [or woman] takes the drink, then the drink takes a drink, then the drink takes the man."*
>
> Old Japanese saying

Everyone who has a problem with drinking too much has a story to tell, and I would like to tell you about my experience. You'll probably be able to relate to at least some of it.

One of my earliest memories is of my dad coming home drunk at night after the pub closed. He worked as a laborer and had a wife and six children to support. He worked all day until about 5:00p.m., and then he headed straight for the pub.

Most nights, he would arrive back home either drunk or really drunk and would start shouting and swearing for his dinner. This dinner had to be placed on his lap and his cup of tea placed within easy reach. If the dinner was not ready or there was something wrong with it, he would start screaming abusive words at my mother. I hear the words "muck, fucking muck" ringing in my ears to this day.

In an effort to keep the peace and calm him down, my mother would run after him and do everything that she could to please him. He would eat his dinner and eventually fall asleep on the chair. My mother would sigh with relief.

As I write this it, reminds me of the fairy tale *Jack and the Beanstalk* when the ogre comes in and the wife does all she can to keep the peace. For me and my brothers and sister - and of course my mother - this was a living nightmare. This horrible situation was caused by one thing only: alcohol.

My dad earned about £30 a week, and he gave my mother £17 to take care of the family. Not bad, eh? This had to include the best of butcher meat for my dad, whilst our staple diet consisted mainly of cheap meat pies. Honestly! He got paid on Fridays, and by Wednesdays, he was "borrowing" money from my mother so that he could go to the pub and not have to miss a night.

We were in debt and often couldn't afford to put money in the meter for electricity. I remember that we had an old black and white television that only showed one channel; we couldn't afford to get it fixed.

I sound as if I grew up in the Dark Ages instead of the sixties! We had to rely on the horrible man who came to the house to give us a credit note that we could spend in the overpriced shop he was working for. This same agent managed to sell my mother a football rug for our fireside at a time when we had been issued with an eviction order. He knew we were poor. He lived across the road from us. I remember once when I was about 14, this man got me on my own and tried to touch my breast. I steered clear of him after that, but I was left with lasting feeling of hate and resentment in my heart that I still struggle with even today.

So my dad drank alcohol and made my childhood miserable; why on Earth was I drawn to the stuff? Did I think that alcohol was going to give me the kind of power that my dad enjoyed? I don't know, but I was keen to try it. I was also a very shy child. As I said, we were a poor, large family. I was very aware that people looked down their noses at us. They judged us by the way we were dressed and no doubt by the amateur haircuts we were all given. So after a bit of reflection, I think I probably wanted to drink to help with confidence issues too.

In those days - the "olden days" as my daughters call them - you could take your own bottle to the local shop and get it filled with draught sherry. The cheapest option! I think that this was my first experience with alcohol: sweet and sticky. I always wanted my dad to bring me a little bottle of Babycham for my New Year. I really loved the advertisement with the little deer and the posh glass.

I was always a romantic, I think, searching for (but never finding) the perfect Christmas or New Year. I never did get the Babycham from my dad. Perhaps he knew that he was trapped and didn't want to encourage me down the same path. I will never know, as he never spoke to me unless he was drunk.

When I was 16, I started going out with my first real boyfriend. We went to a pub and he bought me cider and Babycham. Yes, I got my Babycham at last. Strong, sweet alcohol - a powerful combination for someone who weighed less than 110 pounds at the time! I also drank vodka and orange and have, to this day, a vivid recollection of being sick outside of the pub. Violently sick!

I can still remember the vile taste in my mouth and the bright orange mess scattered everywhere, including all over me! (Sorry for being so graphic.) There are some things that you will always remember in detail, like the birth of your children, and this is one horrible memory that will never leave me.

You will notice that my first drinks were quite sweet. Think back to your first drink. Did you have to force it down? The reality is that alcohol tastes horrible and is an acquired taste. The makers of the first alcopops knew that they would be onto something big when they launched this sweet, bright, in-your-face drink. Easy to drink and easy to come back for more - what a combination!

When I first started drinking, I had to invent ways of making this bitter pill of alcohol more bearable. Now alcohol manufacturers have done this for us and make a good profit while they're at it.

It was not until many years later that dry wine

became my drink of choice.

I recall going to a cheese and wine disco in the seventies with my boyfriend and another couple. The wine was "free" once you had paid for your ticket. If someone had given me a glass of vinegar, I wouldn't have been able to tell the difference! It tasted awful, but it was alcohol, so I drank it anyway. I drank it as if it were going out of style. Later that evening, I have a vague recollection of something being stuffed down my throat and me struggling. I ended up comatose.

My friends had called an ambulance, and a doctor or nurse was now washing out my stomach. In the morning, I had to leave the hospital wearing the clothes from the night before - a white skirt and top covered in dried vomit - and make my way home on the bus. I was attending college at the time and had to hand in an assignment that day.

What can I say? Words fail me. This incident, although embarrassing and humiliating, did not stop me from drinking. I used to think that I could never get addicted to alcohol because I suffered so badly from hangovers. How wrong can a person be?

As the years went on, I got married and drank "normally" about twice a week. My husband did not enjoy cans of lager, only pints would do, so we only drank in pubs at first. It was not until I started my family that I started drinking in the house. I had now graduated from cider and Babycham to bottles of wine, as this was more readily available in supermarkets. We didn't have anyone to babysit for us, so we couldn't go out to the pub very much. We just drifted into having a drink at home; it was the easy option.

I'm getting upset as I'm writing this and recalling how shallow my life was. Get the kids into bed and have a drink. Oh my goodness! The number of times I woke up feeling like death warmed up and had to get the kids ready for school then get myself off to work! It was a nightmare. Yet I continued to do this to myself for years.

It didn't start off being every night, but it slowly increased over the years until at one point, I was drinking every night. My daughters were about high school age at that point. I kept my alcoholic drinking hidden from them, pretending that I was a social drinker.

I would drink so much that I would sometimes not make it to bed. I used to fall asleep on the floor on a regular basis. Eventually one bottle of wine was not enough, and I started to drink whatever alcohol I could find in the house. I hated lager, but I could and would drink anything when I was inebriated.

I would wake up in the morning, full of remorse and self-loathing, determined not to put myself through this pain again. This resolve would usually last only a few days at the most, and then I would be buying another bottle of wine, drinking whatever I could find, or jumping in the car and buying another bottle at our local shop.

I think one of the worst things I managed to do was to find champagne that had been given to my daughters for a special occasion, like a birthday or graduation, thinking in my drunken state that I would replace it the next day. I would usually wake up in the morning with no recollection of what I had done the night before or the level to which I had sunk!

Sometimes I would drink red wine. I preferred the full-bodied kind, and I would check that the alcohol content was at least 13% proof. However, the problem with red wine was that it gave me worse hangovers than usual.

I can recall spending entire days in bed just trying to feel better after knocking back a bottle or two of vino rouge! I would have pounding, migraine-like headaches that were unbearable, but I continued drinking it for a long time. It finally dawned on me that I couldn't tolerate the pain of this hangover any longer and resolved not to drink red wine again!

At another point in my drinking career, I can remember sitting and being freezing cold on my front doorstep for some reason, and then actually wetting myself. Oh my goodness! I try hard to blot out that memory, I can tell you.

I can recall another time when I was visiting my sister-in-law, and we decided to light her outside brazier, a sort of open metal fireplace. I got plastered and was walking up and down past this blazing fire. Luckily I didn't injure myself, because I could have easily fallen onto it at any time. Did the realization of what could have happened to me bring me to my senses? Not at all! I just didn't think about it and carried on.

Eventually my eldest daughter noticed that I had a problem with drinking too much and at times expressed her concern to me. I got all defensive and annoyed - the typical response of a problem drinker in denial - but I absolutely knew in my heart that she was right. The result was that I became careful about what I drank around her because I didn't enjoy the hard time she gave me, and I didn't want to upset her.

That's another thing about alcohol - it makes you into a scheming, devious person. I used to call my daughter early in the evening, before I had a drink, to make sure she wouldn't call me later on in the evening and realize that I had been drinking. I used to think about whether it was okay for me to have a drink or not. I would take several factors into consideration. Who was around? Who was going to be around? Who might call? I would need to make sure that I stayed off Facebook because that was a dead giveaway. I sometimes even took the phone off the hook.

My friend who drinks too much has to make sure that she writes everything down if she calls someone, because she usually has no recollection of her conversation the next day! We drinkers have to become very inventive and use lots of strategies to hide our addiction.

Another thing I've tried in the attempt to control my drink is to change what I drink. It doesn't work. It is the nature of alcohol, or any drug, to make moderation very difficult to sustain.

I recently found a great quote by Aaron Howard:

> *"Responsible drinking?*
> *Now that is an oxymoron."*

I am also brilliant at making up excuses to have a drink. I would often say that I had run out of something and would just run to the store to buy more. Of course I would just happen to pick up a bottle of wine too.

My friend picks up these bargain dinner deals which include a bottle of wine. This is a smokescreen. She might not even particularly like the type of meal on sale, but what the heck - if she can have a reason for ending up with a bottle of wine that she will just have to drink, she'll do it.

So that is the rough history of my life with alcohol.

Pathetic really!

Can you relate to some of this? Do you feel hurt and shame when you think about where alcohol has taken you?

Are you ready to get your real life back? The life that you were meant to enjoy and be proud of?

I am not a typical alcoholic; I think that my diagnosis would be a functioning alcoholic. Alcohol has caused me real pain in my life. I suspect that there are thousands upon thousands of people who can tell a similar story. I live in a nice house in a desirable part of town. I hold down a responsible job and have done so for more years than I care to remember. No-one at my place of employment would suspect that I have ruined my life with alcohol. I am in a loving, long-term relationship and have raised my three daughters without them ending up in care. They have all graduated from college, have good jobs, and are doing well for themselves.

I have never drunk in the morning and have always had some measure of control. In some ways, this makes the choice to stop drinking alcohol so much harder because I have not ended up in the gutter, without money or a place to stay. I have not landed in jail because I was caught drinking and driving. I have not reached the proverbial "rock bottom."

My decision to stop drinking has been a difficult one, but the bottom line is that I cannot control alcohol. Alcohol controls me, when I give it a foothold. It was hard giving it up - at least when I was under the impression that I was giving up something good.

When I made the decision to stop drinking, I made the decision to give up the one thing that was causing me real pain and hurt. If you get your mindset right, then you will see that giving up alcohol is the best feeling in the world. You can still enjoy your life. In fact, you will enjoy it more; I promise you.

BEST OF ALL,
YOU WILL BE FREE!

If you have problems in your life because of alcohol, as I have had, then this book might help you to see what the truth about alcohol really is and how your life will definitely be much better without it.

Lots of people have stopped drinking and are reaping the benefits, and you can too if you want to. Best of all, you can have a happy, joyful life without alcohol - *and* you can still have fun! I can honestly say that before I stopped drinking, I could never envision a life without alcohol, far less a happy, joyful life full of real happiness.

So don't just read this book and skim over its message; try to really believe that leading a sober, happy life is possible and that there are thousands upon thousands of people all over the world who have stopped drinking and are leading happier, more fulfilled lives.

I want you to know that if I can stop drinking and enjoy my life, then I know it's possible for you to do the same.

Can you relate to this?

You want a drink, but you know that if you have a drink, you will probably drink too much and then do or say something that you'll regret. You will spend the whole next day feeling hellish because of your self-inflicted hangover, and you will probably have a host of other miserable regrets.

Do you envy "normal drinkers"? Normal drinkers are the kind of people who can take or leave a drink - the ones who can leave a glass of wine or beer and go to bed without a second thought.

Would you like to be able to go and have a few drinks with your friends and then be able to walk home remembering what you have done the next morning with no feelings of guilt or shame?

Have you tried to do this but end up drinking too much anyway, not wanting to stop? Have you ended up wrecking your mental and physical heath again?

Do you love alcohol but at the same time hate it and its power over you?

Have you ever tried to escape its grip and ended back in the same old sorry state?

Do you realize just how much peace and freedom that you would have in your life if you were able to pull away from its grip?

I will repeat what you would gain - **PEACE** and **FREEDOM**. This truth took a long time to penetrate my brain, but when I finally "got it," my life improved in so many ways! As I write these words, I hope that you too can find happiness without alcohol.

When you really have had enough and want your life, freedom, peace of mind, and energy back, how can you convince yourself that drinking alcohol is bad for you and no longer an option? For some, it may be helpful to put alcohol in the BAD HEALTH category, like cigarettes.

Because remember, it is like a ticking time bomb; you never know when you may make a poor decision when you're under the influence that might affect your future negatively.

Do you feel that you need help but that there's *no way* that you are an alcoholic? You would rather die than even think about going to an AA meeting?

You would find it difficult to tell your **best friend** about your drinking problem, far less a room full of strangers!

You just drink too much sometimes and want a drink when everyone else has had enough and wants to go home. You want to have some control. Now for the bad news - this is the point when you might put this book down and feel angry and frustrated.

Alcohol is not your friend and cannot be controlled.

I would like a penny for every person who has tried to control their alcohol intake and failed! The truth of the matter is that alcohol is a strong force, and when allowed into the body, it will rule and ruin your life; **but** if you say no and mean no, it will eventually shrivel up and die. You can tame the monster.

ALCOHOL IS EVERYWHERE!

Drinking alcohol is just so much a part of our culture. Alcohol, especially when you are trying to stop, seems to be absolutely everywhere. When was the last time you took part in one of these activities without seeing alcohol or without alcohol being involved?

Television - Especially soaps! Yet only the very occasional storyline is about people who have problems with their drinking! This is really amazing.

> **Movies** - It would be difficult to find any movie that does not have scenes involving alcohol (except for some movies specifically made for children).

> **Supermarkets** - They make it so easy to buy booze cheaply and, for the quiet problem drinker, anonymously.

> **Birthday parties** - Another year older? Celebrate or drown your sorrows as you hit another milestone. Birthday cards often have a

bottle of champagne on the front, and many mention getting drunk as way of celebrating.

➤ **Weddings** - Have a drink for Dutch courage before the wedding ceremony and then at various points during the reception.

➤ **Retirement parties** - This is another reason to have a drink. If you are the one retiring, you will now have more time to drink and recover from the hangover!

➤ **Funerals** - People use alcohol to toast the life of the newly departed and to drown out the pain of bereavement.

➤ **Graduations** - We use alcohol to celebrate graduating from college!

➤ **Weekends** - We look forward to celebrating the end of the working week with alcohol.

➤ **Barbeques** - For some, this is just an excuse to get legless in the sun.

➤ **Christmas** - It just wouldn't be Christmas without alcohol, now would it?

➤ **New Year's** – Who ever heard of bringing in the New Year without a drink?

➤ **Holidays** - That's what holidays are all about, aren't they? You see people sitting with a pint of beer or a glass of wine at 7:00 a.m. waiting for their flight. Their time in the sun would not be complete without alcohol.

➤ **Restaurants** - You have to taste the wine before you order. How many people ever turn their nose up at the taste or refuse to accept the bottle offered?

> **Dinner parties** - Here you'll find plenty of different wines to go with every course.

The list is endless, and as I said before, the minute that you make the decision to stop drinking, it will seem as if someone is conspiring against you, as you will get invitations right, left, and center. You will also notice people drinking everywhere!

As I am writing this, my daughter's friends have visited unexpectedly with bottles of wine. They will be going out to the pub soon, and I have just refused the offer of a glass of wine and an invitation to join them.

If I had accepted the drink and invitation, I would not be feeling mentally or physically well at all in the morning. The problem is that it is still tempting for a split second. Then, thankfully, sanity takes over, and I am so grateful that I have reached this mindset.

THE ROAD TO MISERY

I fought the battle - with my sensible, sober side fighting against my addicted, drunken side - for years. In order to convince myself that drinking alcohol was only the road to misery, I made a list of all the bad points.

This is what I wrote:

My choices if I continue to drink alcohol. What drinking is doing to me and will continue to do if I carry on drinking.

I am wasting my life.

I am often ill because of drinking.

I am more disorganized.

I become lazier.

I lose motivation.

I lack persistence.

I put on weight.

I find it even more difficult to stick to a diet.

I do not exercise as much.

I feel guilty and wonder what I have done or

whom I have offended whilst drinking.

I go round in circles with my life, getting nowhere fast.

My house becomes a mess, and it is a monumental task to clean it up.

I give my husband a hard time.

I do the bare minimum at work. All I want to do is get home and recover in front of the television.

I spend a fortune, not only on alcohol but also on takeout food and eating out more because I cannot be bothered with cooking after I've had a drink. I also spend more money in pubs because I become very generous when drunk.

I do not attend to my bills properly.

I tend to bury my head in the sand about issues.

Alcohol is a depressant, and it makes me feel generally really low.

MY ESCAPE – THE ANSWER

I asked myself, "Why do I want to continue drinking?"

Logically, drinking had brought me only pain. The pleasure of drinking was just a deception. So why was it so difficult for me to see that alcohol gave me absolutely nothing?

Why was it so difficult for me to see that alcohol only took good things from me?

It took my self-respect, my money, and my health. If alcohol were a person and did this, I would expect that person to be locked up!

What kept me coming back for more? Why was it so difficult for me to break free? Here is the answer.

I always thought that I would be giving something up!

The day I became free of alcohol was the day that I fully understood and embraced the truth that *I would not be giving anything up by not drinking.*

You will be free when you can allow that thought to permeate your brain and your whole being! **You will be giving up nothing**!

The truth

Since stopping, my life has improved in so many ways. I have found peace from a thing that was tearing my life apart, slowly but surely.

One of the biggest advantages that I have found is not having my life ruled by alcohol.

I don't have to think about it anymore!

You would not believe the peace that I have found. It is total bliss. The freedom I have now is amazing.

You see, every night, I would have this argument with myself about whether I was going to have a drink or not and then how much to buy. When I drank, I didn't want to stop, so when I was sober, I bought only a limited quantity of wine. I do not have that pain to deal with now. I don't have to tell my husband to answer the phone because I don't want anyone to find out that I've been drinking again. I also do not have to worry about calling different people when I've had a few and then worrying about what I said to them.

I do not have to spend a fortune on taxis to get home or argue with my husband about whose turn it is to drive. He insisted on my taking my turn to drive in an effort to curb my drinking. He used to drink many years ago and now cannot really be bothered with it. I must admit that the fact that he can now take it or leave it helps me greatly. It would be so much more difficult if he were still drinking.

I enjoy my food better and can control my weight. I am longer taking in empty calories in the form of alcohol. If you think about it, a bottle of wine has about 800 calories. This is a huge chunk of your daily allowance if you are trying to lose weight. Of course, many really good diets exclude alcohol, at least for the initial phase, or only allow a small amount at most.

Not having to drink or think about drinking is like being released from a prison. All the time, **I held the key** but didn't know how to use it. Well now I have the key, and I am never letting it go.

SAVE MONEY

STOP DRINKING - GET RICH BY THE POWER OF COMPOUND INTEREST!

One of the big advantages of stopping drinking is the amount of money that you will be able to save.

I figured out that by the time I had bought my bottles of wine and wasted money on fast food (because I wasn't fit to cook) I was saving myself an average of £60 a week! That's more than $90.

Why would I take all of my hard-earned money and pour it down the drain just to waste my life and feel lousy the next day? What is the point?

So I decided to take that money and put it into a savings account every week before I got used to having it in my pocket again!

You have probably heard the famous quote attributed to Albert Einstein:

> **"Compound interest is the 8th wonder of the world."**

Well it's true. It is amazing. Saving £60 a week might not seem like much, but with the power of compound interest, it can add up to a small fortune over time. It would be £240 in just 4 weeks, and throughout a year, it would add up to an incredible £3,120. That's more than $4,700 USD. In just 10 years, you will have a big pile of cash that has accumulated interest and then interest on the interest!

I calculated the actual amount using an online compound interest savings, assuming a modest rate of interest of 4%. The total came to £35,222 ($53,840.35)! If I based my calculation on a 20-year term, then I would be sitting on a juicy **£87,608 ($133,917.59)!!** I don't know about you, but this is a big motivating factor for me!

Get a piece of paper and a pen and calculate how much you spend daily, weekly, and monthly on alcohol. Make sure that you include all the extra money that you spend because you were drunk or hung-over. This might include:

- ➢ Food you buy when you just have to have something to eat after drinking.
- ➢ Food you have to throw out because you were too ill to cook it before it expired.
- ➢ Eating out because you cannot be bothered with cooking.

> Days lost at work.
> Items you bought that you didn't need but thought you did when you were under the influence of alcohol.

You will be able to think of other ways your money is squandered too. Write it all down and add it up. You will be shocked. However, now you can start planning what you can do with all of the money that you will save when you stop drinking.

Change your thinking, and you'll change your life!

By changing the way I looked at alcohol, I was able to walk away from it.

When I finally realized that alcohol gave me nothing at all except sadness and misery, I was able to leave it behind.

Let me ask you a very important question. This should not be skipped over. Take your time to really give it some thought.

CAN YOU IMAGINE GETTING SOBER, OR DO YOU IMMEDIATELY THINK OF FAILING?

You have to be able to see yourself living a life without alcohol. You have to change your thinking about alcohol, and if you do, you can change your life for the better. Just get it clear in your mind about how much alcohol has cost you and your family.

You also need to forgive yourself for anything that you have done when you have been drunk. You will have to nurture the mindset that **you will do whatever it takes to get sober and stay sober.** Do not resent your decision, but instead use your willpower and give yourself a chance to be all that you can be.

Make yourself and the people that you care about proud. If there are people that you love and care about having similar problems with alcohol, you could motivate yourself to help them too by setting the example of how good life can be without alcohol. But mainly do this for yourself!

> *"Walk away from the 97% crowd.*
> *Don't use their excuses.*
> *Take charge of your own life."*
>
> Jim Rohn

One of the things that people worry about when they've made the decision to stop drinking is losing their drinking buddies. You know, the friends you socialize with on a regular basis - you enjoy their company when you are having a beer or sharing a bottle or two, but how will that friendship be affected when you tell them you no longer drink? Should you still socialize with them, or will they be a true friend and accept your decision?

Often, although it does not seem like it, people will be jealous that you have made the decision to break away from the destructive effects of alcohol. They don't want you to stop because that leaves them vulnerable. They already know in their heart of hearts that drinking is not good for them, and now you are making them think about it more. Be aware of friends trying to talk you out of your decision.

> *"Drunkenness is nothing but voluntary madness."*
>
> Seneca

YOU ARE GIVING UP NOTHING. YOU HAVE NOTHING TO LOSE AND EVERYTHING TO GAIN.

The term *giving up* implies that you are going to be losing out on something if you stop drinking. Believe me: the only thing that you will be giving up on is misery.

Some people say that drinking is their only pleasure in life. If this is what you believe, then you need to start doing more with your life. Alcohol is expensive, so why not channel this money into giving yourself a different type of high? Treat yourself to a massage or go watch your favorite team playing. Find out what your non-drinking friends do to entertain themselves.

People believe that alcohol makes them happy. How happy are you when you wake up in the morning wishing that you could turn the clock back? When you are trying desperately to remember what you did the night before - did you get in your car and drive?

Are you looking around in the morning, trying to work out where you are and how you got there? Do you even remember that "happy" time that alcohol gave you?

I know from my experience with drinking that the price I had to pay for this elusive happiness was far too high. Alcohol did not make me truly happy.

We believe that alcohol gives us confidence. Well in some ways I would agree with this statement, but let us think about it more closely. You have a drink because you need confidence. Under the influence of alcohol, you are likely to end up making a complete fool of yourself. You will feel more confident that you can drive home from a night out. You will feel more confident that you can call someone up and tell them what you think of them or someone else.

Some people might feel so confident after lubricating themselves that they physically attack another person. They might become so confident that they go out and leave their children alone in the house whilst they go out for more alcohol. You may bring up subjects with your family and friends that you were afraid to bring up before.

However, to successfully manage this confidence, you will need tact and compassion. This is something that is not possible under the influence of alcohol. People will see that you have been drinking, unless they have been drinking themselves, and really resent your drunken intervention.

More than once I've been told, "I am not having this

conversation with you when you are drunk!" Confidence should come from respecting yourself and building your self-esteem, not from a bottle of alcohol.

We may be under the impression that we can never enjoy ourselves without alcohol. I have a friend who does not drink. She sees no point in it. She tells me that when she is out for the evening that she wants to give the person she is speaking to the honor of being mentally present for them so that she can really listen and respond meaningfully to them.

The next time that you are out somewhere and alcohol is involved, take a few minutes to look around. You will spot at least one person who is away in a world of their own. You will also see and hear drunken, emotionally-charged conversations that no-one will remember the next morning. If they do manage to remember, chances are that they will not like what they remember.

Ask yourself if they are enjoying themselves. I apologize, but there's a rant coming up now. This is pointless, pointless, pointless and a ridiculous way to waste your precious life!! We have a saying where I live, and you will probably be able to think of something similar: "Be happy while you're living, for you're a long time dead." So make the most of your life. Now! Today!

Even although we know - absolutely know - that drinking is bad for us on so many levels, we do not want to let it go. Our addicted side is holding on for grim death. Our sober side fights to keep our sanity.

The struggle continues. We remember the well-worn definition of insanity:

> *"If we keep doing what we are doing, we will keep getting what we are getting."*

But guess what? We just keep repeating the same actions over and over again with the same outcome.

> *"It is like gambling somehow. You go out for a night of drinking and you don't know where you are going to end up the next day. It could end up good or it could be disastrous. It's like the throw of the dice."*
>
> Jim Morrison

Jim was a member of 'The Doors' and died at the age of 27 due to addiction.

DRINKING HAS ALWAYS CAUSED US PROBLEMS

In the nineteenth century, this guy named Samuel Blythe wrote about his decision to quit drinking. He had been drinking all of his life and was now weighing the pros and cons of what stopping drinking would mean for him.

This is what he wrote.

> "Here is the way it totted up against quitting. Practically every friend you have in the United States, and you've got a lot of them, drink more or less. You have not cultivated any other line of associates. If you quit drinking, you will necessarily have to quit a lot of these friends, and quit their parties and company because a man who doesn't drink is always a death's-head at a feast or merrymaking where drinking is going on.

Your social intercourse with these people is predicated on taking an occasional drink, in going to places where drinks are served, both public and at homes. The kinds of drinking you do makes greatly for sociability, and you are a sociable person and like to be round with congenial people. You will miss a lot of fun; a lot of good, clever companionship, for you are too old to form a new line of friends. Your whole game is organized along these lines. Why make a hermit of yourself just because you think drinking may harm you? Cut it down. Take care of yourself. Don't be such a fool as to try to change your manner of living just when you have an opportunity to live as you should and enjoy what is coming to you.

This is the way it lined up for quitting: So far, liquor hasn't done anything to you except cause you to waste some time that might have been otherwise employed; but it will get you, just as it has landed a lot of your friends, if you stay by it. Wouldn't it be better to miss some of this stuff you have come to think of as fun, and live longer? There is no novelty in drinking to you. You haven't an appetite that cannot be checked, but you will have if you stick to it much longer. Why not quit and take a chance at a new mode of living, especially when you know absolutely that every health reason, every future-prospect reason, every atom of good sense in you, tells you there is nothing to be gained by keeping at it, and that all may be lost?

Well, I pondered over that a long time. I had watched miserable wretches who had struggled to stay on the water wagon - sometimes with amusement. I knew what they had to stand if they tried to associate with their former companions; I knew the apparent difficulties and the disadvantages of this new mode of life. On the other hand, I was convinced that, so far as I was concerned, without trying to lay down a rule for any other man, I would be an ass if I didn't quit it immediately, while I was well and all right, instead of waiting until I had to quit on a doctor's orders, or got to that stage when I couldn't quit.

It was no easy thing to make the decision. It is hard to change the habits and associations of twenty years! I had a good understanding of myself. I was no hero. I liked the fun of it, the companionship of it, better than anyone. I like my friends and, I hope and think that they like me. It seemed to me that I needed it in my business, for I was always dealing with men who did drink.

I wrestled with it for some weeks. I thought it all out, up one side and down the other. Then I quit. Also I stayed quit. And believe me, ladies and gentlemen and all others present, it was no fool of a job.

Sizing it up, one side against the other, I conclude that it is better for me not to drink. I find I have much more time that I can devote to my business; that I think more clearly, feel better, do not make any loose statements under the exhilaration of alcohol, and keep my mind on my number constantly. The item of time is the surprising item. It is astonishing how much time you have to do things in that formerly you used to drink in, with the accompaniment of all the piffle that goes with drinking! When you are drinking you are never too busy to take a drink and never too busy not to stop. You are busy all the time, but get nowhere. Work is the curse of the drinking classes."

REASONS FOR HANGING ON TO ALCOHOL

One of the main reasons that we hang on to alcohol for dear life, even though we know that it is really hurting us in so many ways, is our belief that we are giving something up. We talk about having to "give up drinking" as if we are really going to be losing something.

Getting our mindset right here will often be the difference between success and failure. We have to get it firmly established in our mind, brain, body, and soul that we are not giving anything up. Nothing! Nothing! Nothing! Indeed, as soon as we make the decision to stop drinking, our life will only get better and better.

When you're doubting your ability to stop drinking, these excuses may come to mind about alcohol:

- ➤ It gives me confidence.
- ➤ It relieves my stress.
- ➤ It helps me relax.
- ➤ I would lose all my friends.

> ➤ I would not know what to do with myself.
> ➤ My partner drinks.

When I was drinking, I used to try to scare myself into stopping drinking. You know, by making a list of all the bad effects of alcohol. This list would include:

> ➤ Putting on weight
> ➤ Becoming more depressed
> ➤ Spending a fortune

I think that we problem drinkers somehow hate ourselves in an odd sort of way. Why else would we continually poison and hurt our minds and bodies? I sometimes thought that perhaps subconsciously I was hurting myself with alcohol on purpose. It was a way of reinforcing my deeply held belief that I was not good enough and would never be good enough. This is why it is so vitally important to improve our self-esteem and work on it daily.

HEALTH PROBLEMS

I know a woman who used to be drop-dead gorgeous when she was younger - until alcohol got a grip on her. Her cute nose is now bulbous and red. Her lovely complexion is now marred by redness, and her eyes are constantly bloodshot. She has never been short of a man in her life until now. She is painfully thin. With the help of makeup, she can look barely presentable, but when she sits in front of the mirror at the end of the day and takes her makeup off, she must want to cry. Alcohol has savaged her and is ruling her life, yet she still drinks daily. She is alcohol dependant. Not a roaring drunk, but someone whose life is quietly dominated by alcohol!

The power of alcohol is that it creeps upon us, slowly and silently. The first stage might be that we are aware that we are drinking too much and have tried to cut down our intake. We might say "I won't have another drink until Friday" or "I will not start drinking until my children are in bed or after 8:00 p.m." The next thing we will become aware of - and hate - is friends and family complaining about our drinking or giving us friendly advice that we do not want or feel that we need.

We then get defensive and angry. We start to notice how much other people are drinking to help make ourselves feel better about the amount that we are drinking. I used to find myself looking in peoples' shopping baskets at the supermarket. It seemed to help me in some bizarre way. I would think to myself, "I'm not that bad. Look at her with that huge bottle of vodka and all of those bottles of wine."

I have a friend who always comments the next day if one of his friends has had too much the night before. He drinks every night and often to excess. He is trying to make himself feel better. I do not condemn him; I feel sorry for him, even though I know that this sounds patronizing. I know that he is not ready at this point in his life to face his drinking problem and would probably laugh in my face if I said anything to him. It's likely he was projecting unconscious self-loathing about his own drinking onto his friends. You see, you have to realize that you are having problems with alcohol before you have any chance of beating it.

Acceptance of the problem is a huge step toward solving it.

We do not want to believe that we cannot control alcohol and that alcohol is, in truth, controlling and dictating our lives. When you free yourself of a dictator, like alcohol, the freedom that you experience is totally amazing and so empowering. You get your life back.

THINGS THAT HAVE HELPED ME TO ESCAPE

TAKING RESPONSIBILITY FOR MY LIFE

Looking back over my early life, I realize that I have, in the past, blamed my drinking on my upbringing or other issues like lack of confidence. I have discovered that in order to improve my life, I have to stop blaming circumstances. I must take 100% responsibility for my life.

You need to do the same. Forgive people who you think have caused or helped aggravate your problems.

> *"Resentment is like taking poison and waiting for the other person to die."*
>
> M. McCourt

In truth, these "reasons" are just excuses. So step up and decide that you will not give your power away to anyone.

You will keep it for yourself and channel it to take

you where you really want to go.

UNDERSTANDING MY LOW SELF-ESTEEM

As I mentioned earlier, low self-esteem is something that affects many people; chances are that people who drink too much on a regular basis will probably have big issues with this, but they might not even be aware of it.

I know that I was coming from a place of low self-esteem due in part to my upbringing. It was as if I did not really love myself properly.

Subconsciously I had been taught that I was not of much significance, growing up with a father who had no time for me and never once - no exaggeration here - gave me any kind of compliment or sober attention.

Can you relate to any of this?

BOOSTING YOUR SELF-ESTEEM WILL HELP YOU QUIT DRINKING

Holding negative beliefs about yourself lowers your resilience and ability to cope with the stresses of life.

When you have that feeling of not being able to cope, you just want to damp down those feelings. And what is the quickest, easiest, short-term solution? Yes, just have a drink, and to hell with the consequences. The result is short-term relief but long-term misery!

Here are some things you can do to raise your self-esteem and make yourself feel better.

- Don't put yourself down. Ever!
- Stop comparing yourself to other people. There will always be people out there who are slimmer, richer, etc. than you, and that's okay.
- Get into the habit of thinking and saying positive things *about* yourself *to* yourself. Look in the mirror, smile, and give yourself a compliment.
- Accept compliments from other people.
- Use self-help books and websites to help you change your beliefs. Brian Tracy is my favorite author. Check out his books on Amazon.
- Spend your time with positive, supportive people. Steer clear of people who are negative or put you down.
- Accept your positive qualities and things you are good at.
- Be assertive; don't allow people to treat you with a lack of respect.
- Make a list of all the great things that you have in your life.

STOPPING OR CONTROLLING ALCOHOL

It is extremely difficult to control alcohol because as soon as you take it into your system, it immediately gets the upper hand! It is like fighting against your arch enemy, and then as soon as the battle has started, you go and give all your weapons to the opposing side. Then what are your chances of coming out unscathed and victorious?

I know that when I take one drink, it will be one drink too many. One drink is too much, and a thousand is not enough, as the old saying goes.

The addicted brain and the sober brain fight for the upper hand in a person who has problems with alcohol. The addict has this continual fight going on. Part of him wants to keep drinking no matter where it leads him, whilst the other part is screaming to get free!

The addiction part is strong and will often overpower the sober self. However, the sober self can be triumphant. We need to nourish the part of us that wants to be sober and let the addicted side of us die.

TOOLS THAT CAN HELP YOU

You have to use all of the tools you possibly can if you want to succeed. Here is one that I find really useful and still use regularly to help with various problems.

This technique has been used successfully to treat war veterans who have developed post-traumatic stress disorder, so you can see how powerful it is.

EMOTIONAL FREEDOM TECHNIQUE

In the last few years, I have made a remarkable discovery. You may have heard of it, as it is gaining in popularity. It is known as the Emotional Freedom Technique, or EFT for short.

If you're searching for freedom from addiction, increased self-esteem, more confidence, more money, more energy, more abundance, more peace - more anything positive - or relief from anxiety and stress, then I recommend that you give this unbelievably powerful technique a try.

Not only is it amazingly effective, but it is a very simple technique that can be learned in minutes and used to improve all areas of your life. And I mean *all* areas!

This useful tool, commonly known as tapping, can help you relieve stress in your life and help you cope

when you are feeling weak against alcohol
simple to learn and do, but it is also
powerful. It is based on the ancient Chinese art of
acupuncture, just without the needles. Do not let the
simplicity of this method fool you, as you can use this
method **any time** to help you in the comfort of your
own home. It really can help.

You need to start by stating what the problem is. For
example:

> ***Even though I feel stressed and need a drink,***
> ***I deeply and completely accept and forgive***
> ***myself without judgment.***

(This is the statement.)

While you are saying the statement, tap lightly on the
side of your hand, using four fingers. This is best
described as your "karate chop" area.

Repeat your statement three times, with feeling.

Now tap the top of your head and say ***"This stress."***

Move now to the edge of your eyebrow, just above
your nose, and tap on this point, saying, ***"This
stress."***

Now move to the side of your eye. Tap lightly and
say, ***"This stress."***

Follow the sequence and continue tapping lightly on
these areas:

  ➢ Under your eye
  ➢ Under your nose

49

- ➤ Under your mouth
- ➤ On your collar bone
- ➤ Under your arm
- ➤ Back to the top of your head again

Repeat this sequence at least three times. At the end, take a deep breath and breathe out.

I must warn you that because you are releasing blocked up energy, you may become very emotional. You may cry. Lots of people, including me, cannot stop yawning when they tap. This is proof that the tapping has a positive impact. Use this technique at least once a day.

It works on many different issues apart from helping with stress. I used to take painkillers at least once a week for headaches. Since using EFT, I have not needed to. This method can also be effective if you suffer from sleep problems. This might be an issue for you when you give up alcohol.

EFT has gained in popularity over the last few years, so you will find lots of information and videos on the Internet about it. I find it helpful to tap along to different videos that I find on YouTube.

I particularly like Brad Yates. He is very easy to follow, and watching someone actually tapping will really help you to get started properly.

For a more in-depth guide to the Emotional Freedom Technique, may I recommend Gary Craig's quick and easy guide. Again, just search for these names online, or you could type in "tapping" or "EFT." This is not a sales pitch, by the way. I have no financial connection to these guys. It's just that their work is amazing. Give this technique a go and watch your life improve!

Although this is a safe method, it can often bring up all kinds of deep-seated emotional trauma that may have been buried away for years. Be aware that this may happen and that you must take full responsibility for your own well-being if you decide to try tapping.

HYPNOSIS

You can do this without hypnosis, but I would recommend downloading an app onto your phone or iPod. There are hypnosis tapes available for all sorts of things, including stress busting and building confidence and self-belief. Many of them are totally free or very inexpensive - certainly not more than the cost of one night of drinking.

You need to give yourself every chance to beat this and set yourself free. Take your decision seriously and take massive action to get your life back on track. Joseph Clough is really good, and many of his recordings are free. Again, just do a Google search.

SUPPORT GROUPS

Here are the names of a few support groups you may be interested in:

> Life Ring
> Alcoholics Anonymous

> ➤ Sober Recovery

You will be able to find brilliant support in your quest to stop alcohol ruining your life by searching the Internet for any of the above. You do not have to attend classes if you don't want to; I just used online support.

It is all free, and you can talk to and get support from people who are going through the same thing or something similar. You also can gain strength from helping and encouraging other people along the way.

CELEBRITIES WHO DON'T DRINK ALCOHOL

> *"It has been almost 12 years since I took a drink and I am still struck by disbelief when I see someone in a restaurant with a half-finished glass of wine near at hand. I want to get up, go over and yell 'Finish that! Why don't you finish that?' into his or her face. I found the idea of social drinking ludicrous – if you didn't want to get drunk why not just have a Coke?"*
>
> Stephen King

I can relate so much to this quote by Stephen King. As a former problem drinker, he still cannot understand why someone would leave an alcoholic drink. Cutting down on what you drink is not an option. It will never solve your problems with alcohol.

When you take your first drink, then it is as if you have lit the blue touch paper. There is no going back. All of your resolve just to have one or two drinks will fly out the window as soon as the effect of your first drink kicks in. It's just a downward spiral from there.

Here is a short list of people in the public eye who have given up alcohol because it became a real problem in their lives; some have always chosen to abstain.

(At the time of writing, this information was, to the best of my knowledge, correct. However, such is the nature of alcohol; any one of the following celebrities may have relapsed. Hopefully not.)

- David Bowie
- Jim Carrey - Well I think he has a fun life without alcohol!
- Eric Clapton
- Alice Cooper
- Rolf Harris
- Robert Downey, Jr.
- Penn Jillette
- Donny Osmond - Due to his religious beliefs, Donny abstains from alcohol.
- Donald Trump
- Elton John - He has said that his life only really started when he stopped drinking.
- Anthony Hopkins
- Bruce Lee
- Rob Lowe - He commented that you have to be ready to stop for yourself and no-one else. I think that this is so true. Yes, your family and friends will benefit big time from your

decision to stop drinking, but ultimately, you must stop drinking for you and because you want to.

- Ewan McGregor - A Scottish actor who has admitted to being a "functioning alcoholic" and a "miserable drunk" in the past and who made the decision to stop drinking.
- Eddie Murphy
- Cristiano Ronaldo
- Stephanie Meyer - She too abstains from alcohol due to religious beliefs.
- George Bernard Shaw
- Donald Trump - He once said, "I tell people, 'What are you drinking for?' And they don't even understand what I'm saying."
- John Travolta
- Bruce Willis
- Sarah Silverman
- Tyra Banks
- Anne Robinson - The star of the hit quiz program "The Weakest Link" stopped drinking many years ago after being told by doctors that she had only 6 weeks to live. At that point, she weighed only 84 pounds.

Check out Wikipedia teetotalers on Google, and you will see a long list of celebrities who either have stopped drinking or have never drunk.

Millions of people are putting up with lives filled with poor health and emotional baggage. Not knowing how to achieve the joyful and satisfying lives they desire, they're stuck accepting a lifestyle of emotional trauma, chronic physical pain, compulsions and addictions, or perhaps just an empty feeling inside.

Along with these problems come pills to kill the pain, to help bring sleep at night, and to suppress anxiety - but these "cures" are sometimes hardly better than the disease. I have known people who live a pitiful excuse for a life because the only help that they have been given are medicines that not only take away their symptoms but in the process take away their motivation and zest for life.

If you're like many people, you feel trapped, caught in this cycle. You're tired of being sad, depressed, anxious, and discontent, never feeling totally well. You're sick of expensive and ineffective treatments. You're fed up with relinquishing power over your health and happiness to psychologists and doctors.

You'd like to grow, thrive, and make the most of your life by putting the past in the past. You want to be your best, living a life that is filled with peace, true joy, and a real sense of fulfillment every single day.

MY STOP-DRINKING BLOG

When I decided to stop drinking, I thought that it might be a good idea to keep a simple blog of my feelings and thoughts in an attempt to inspire and motivate myself. I really found this helpful, so I thought that I would include it here.

I think that doing this made me aware of recurring patterns in my life that had led me back to drinking in the past. Things like feeling bored or feeling that I was missing out on something.

By making myself aware of what I was thinking and the "alcoholic mindset" I was in danger of falling into, I was able to see my thinking for what it really was. I did my very best to cut those negative thoughts running in my head and focus on the positive aspects of stopping drinking.

So here it is. Some days I was just too busy with life to write much of anything. I would recommend that you try this to give you an insight into your own feelings and thoughts. You should also read all of your blog over regularly. This is great therapy for - you'd be charged a great deal of money for this by a professional. When you stop drinking, you have to take **massive action** to change your thinking so that you will be successful in changing your life for the better. It is so easy to forget the problems caused by alcohol. Use every means that you can. This is your life we're talking about!

DAY 1

Well here I am again. Hung over and feeling hellish, again. I cannot put into words just how bad I feel mentally and physically. I need to stop drinking. I wish I could feel exactly like this when I think about buying alcohol. I seem to blank out the pain and the horrible hangover that the next day will, without a shadow of a doubt, bring. I cannot just have one or two. In my brain the only point to drinking is to get happy. Well that is a joke, isn't it? Happy? I have never been so miserable in my life.

Since I started back drinking a year ago, I have become really depressed and have put on over a stone in weight. Not good for someone who is only 5 foot!

I have made a few half-hearted attempts to stop recently but now I really must get my life back. When I come to the end of my life I need to know that I did everything in my power to be the best that I could be.

I must be brave. That is a ridiculous statement of course. You see I still think that I am giving something up!! I find myself looking in people's shopping baskets to see if they are buying alcohol. I ask my friends at work what they drink. Why am I so obsessed with what other people are doing? Is it just to make myself feel better that other people are ruining their life with alcohol too? Yes that is probably what it is. To make me feel that I am not alone in my trap and that there are other idiots wasting their lives too.

So my thinking is that if other people are drinking then it can't be that bad or that there are people who drink more than me, therefore I can't be that bad. I just know that alcohol is doing me no favors at all, and I never want to feel like this again......ever.

DAY 2

It is Sunday morning and no hangover! I love it. I love it. I love it. I am feeling great. I am positive and motivated. I have started writing down my most pressing goals and plan to work through them systematically starting today. The sun is now shining in bonnie Scotland and I have another day off work. Best of all I can enjoy it without a hangover. What more could I ask for?

DAY 3

I had a good, refreshing sleep. Feel good. Feeling strong, but then I always feel strong at the beginning of the week. It is when my working week goes on that I feel that I need to have a drink and then talk myself into it. I do not want to think that 'I deserve a drink' so I must be aware of this danger as the week goes on and take positive steps to combat it.

DAY 4

I had a great night's sleep. Feeling able to cope and pleased with myself. Do not get lulled into a false sense of security.

DAY 5

When I wake up I will feel great! I am making plans to conquer the weekend and not fall into the alcohol trap. It is quite exciting and I cannot wait to have a full weekend off work without feeling lousy. I have got my life back again. It is so exciting!

DAY 6

Danger day!

Alert to self. Just because you have had a 'hard week' and you have an easy day at work tomorrow does not mean that you need or deserve a drink tonight. On the contrary Liz; you need to be good to yourself. You can truly be good to yourself by not drinking and waking up in the morning feeling great with no all-day hangover to ruin your life!

Imagine too the whole weekend feeling good. You are not depriving yourself of anything good. You will be gaining health and self-respect.

DAY 7

I am still feeling on top of the world.

I am going to go to the hairdresser's tonight to treat myself. It will be just as if I am getting it for free because of the money I have saved not giving myself hangovers!

I love it!

DAY 8

I am having a bad day, not because of alcohol but because of a family problem. I am not going to have a drink but I feel stressed. Alcohol is my enemy and I love not having a hangover! Keep remembering this! Make this your mantra and repeat daily.

Alcohol is my enemy!

DAY 9

If I can get through a day like yesterday without a drink, I can get through anything! The situation is not resolved though. I will see what happens today.

It is Sunday morning and I got up at 6 am. No hangover. I love it!

My life is so much better without alcohol.

You know my friends at work talk about how they can't wait for a drink or that they will be opening the wine when they get home. It made me feel that I was not alone in drinking too much. But in reality, their experience of having a good drink was having 2 small glasses of wine and then falling asleep in front of the television.

I have been out with them for the evening and it is amazing how long that they can make one glass last! In the past I was always desperate for another glass - and not a small one either. So desperate that I would make an excuse to go through to where the alcohol was kept and top up my glass. I would then slug this drink down and refill my glass to the same level so that nobody would notice.

One glass was never enough. If I am drinking, I drink to get drunk. Full stop! I drink to oblivion. How pathetic is that? I need to stop now, as I am starting to feel sorry for myself.

This is the best choice that I could ever make.

DAY 10

Well, I have had a terrible weekend that has put a strain on all of the family. I won't go into details, but it has been horrible and it is still ongoing.

Apart from this I have not had a drink, and I feel triumphant and elated.

Everything, including life's problems, are easier to cope with when you are not drinking.

I feel more in control.

I have more energy.

I get things done.

I am saving a ton of money.

I don't wake up cringing when I remember what I did the night before.

I don't have to ask my husband to answer the phone because my daughters will know that I have been drinking and will worry about me.

I have my self-respect.

I can keep control of my weight better.

I can drive at any time of day or night.

My husband does not drink as much - although he is one of those 'lucky' drinkers who can take it or leave it.

This is just a quick list. I could probably write a book on the benefits of not drinking.

DAY 11

Feeling good! My mind is clearer and I do not need to reproach myself about what I have or have not done when I was drunk. This peace and freedom of mind is so precious.

DAY 12

Another brilliant day without alcohol!

I went into my garden this morning and it was really quiet and warm with that smell of summer. This reminds me of peaceful times that I yearn for. I have this fantasy of swimming in a cool, blue lagoon in Hawaii, with the sun warming my back. I have had this longing for years. It would be so wonderful. I think that it goes back to a time when I very young and wanted everything to be perfect. I want to be at peace with myself and my world.

I asked myself why I should choose a drink over this because when I drink I even struggle to get up in the morning and just want the day to be over so that I can feel better again! When I choose alcohol, it's as if I don't really care about myself. I know that I just want to bury emotions and problems too.

Sometimes I think that I really don't like myself at all. I would not sentence my daughters or friends to what I subject myself to. The reason is because I love them and care for them. In short, I want the best for them. If I did pour alcohol down their throats, I would be prosecuted and locked up in jail for a very long time! I need to learn to love myself more. I need to learn how to cherish myself more.

I wonder if this stems back to my childhood when I

did not really get the love and attention that I needed, as there were so many of us. I remember pretending to be ill, because that always got me a little bit more attention. This might be where this feeling of not caring for myself, or loving myself enough stems from.

After all, if you have a dad who spent the majority of the time ignoring your existence, never telling you that you were pretty or that he loved you, and a mother who was too busy with looking after six children by herself it is hardly surprising that I have not learned how to value and love myself properly. I can breathe a sigh of relief that I have been able to instill in my daughters a sense of personal worth that is so needed for every child.

I always, always, always want to see alcohol in its true light, a poison, and a destroyer of self-respect and a waste of life!

Day 13

I am going to start doing more fun things with my life instead of just working, eating, sleeping and watching mind-numbing television.

I have worked it out that I probably save at least £60 a week or more by not drinking, so I could use this to treat myself instead. I find this really hard to do. I can spend money on my family quite easily but always look for the cheapest option for myself or often make do, even though I can afford it. It possibly has something to do with the fact that I was the eldest of 6 and we were poor. The main theme running through the household was "We can't afford it." This has somehow stuck in my brain. It also ties in to the lack of self-worth theory.

Anyway, enough of me feeling sorry for myself! I have to learn to move on and be thankful for all the good things in my life.

I am away to make some good old-fashioned porridge for my breakfast. Apart from the problem over the last week that has not been resolved yet, I am feeling better than I have in a long time. Alcohol is also a depressant and I am so glad that I have stopped.

DAY 14

There is a mini heat wave here in Scotland.

I was reading the book about Life Ring last night; I can't remember what it is called exactly, something with Sobriety in the title. I don't have a physical copy; I have just downloaded it onto my phone.

Anyway it was interesting to read about why AA does not work for everyone. It also has been giving me more of an insight into Life Ring. I must find out more about this.

At last I have been able to lose a little weight without trying too hard. When I was drinking I would really cut my calorie intake so that I could 'treat' myself to wine and still lose weight. WHAT A JOKE!

In reality I would have my allotted amount of wine and then hunt out any other alcohol in the house. I hate the taste of beer but it didn't matter. We have a disgusting saying in Scotland: "He would even drink it through a sh*tty cloot. (A cloot being a piece of material.) I was 'happy' and I wanted to be 'happier'.

When I am writing this I cannot tell you how angry I feel with myself. Not to mention stupid.

I want to cry, not with sadness, but with happiness and thankfulness that I have managed to drag myself out of that degrading Hell.

DAY 15

I have no hangover this morning and am feeling so much better. I feel happier and healthier. I found this great quote.

> *"Disgust and resolve are two of the two great emotions that lead to change."*
>
> Jim Rohn

Well, I can certainly agree with Jim Rohn here. I am sure other drinkers can relate to this feeling too.

DAY 16

I had a lovely day. I went to a lovely little restaurant with my husband and two of my three daughters. My husband had a pint of Guinness and I did not even think about ordering an alcoholic drink. It really is a nice feeling. I hope that I feel like this forever. I want to continue onwards and upwards towards a better life.

DAY 17

This is my seventeenth day of sobriety and I am feeling strong. I feel that I have been surrounded by alcohol recently. The opportunities to drink are everywhere at the moment. I think that this is a bit like when you have bought a new car and you suddenly see them appearing everywhere or when someone tells you not to think of a pink elephant. I hope that I do not begin to feel resentful at a subconscious level.

DAY 18

My 17th day without alcohol completed successfully. I can hardly believe it! I am getting stronger every day. I love this feeling!

Not much to get excited about in terms of time I suppose, BUT the difference is that I have been really and truly enjoying not having alcohol. I realize that it has no place in my life. I want to prove to my family that they do not have to worry about me and alcohol any more. At this moment in time I am 100% sure that my life is so much better without poisoning myself on a regular basis.

I have been in contact with a woman online and we are sharing and confiding our mutual problems with each other. She has just spent some time in jail because she got caught drinking and driving. This has been a real wake-up call for her. It is amazing how much it helps to talk to someone who really can empathize with you and knows exactly where you are coming from. She knows that realistically there is only one course of action that she can take that will totally sort the problem: stop drinking alcohol. She has made that decision and is now is a much better place mentally and physically.

On Friday two people are retiring from work and there is a retirement dinner organized at one of the local hotels. I have already offered to drive so that people will not ask me why I am not having a drink. This is a little bit of a problem for me because I think that if I tell people that I have stopped drinking then I will feel under pressure. It is hard to explain. But then I think to myself that there will be lots of people there on Friday who will not be drinking or hardly drinking at all, so I should just chill.

I feel that my actions will speak louder than my words. This reminds me of the quote by Gandhi: ***"Be the change that you wish to see in the world"*** - or words to that effect. I think that when I have been sober for a year or more I won't feel such a fraud and will be able to say proudly, "No thanks, I don't drink."

I can't wait!

Day 19

Right I need to start getting my life sorted out.

No more drowning problems in alcohol only for them to reappear after I have recovered from my hangover. Today I worked out that the average time I totally wasted when I decided to drink was about 30 hours, made up of 6 hours drinking and 24 hours recovering.

I made a list of all of the negative consequences I inflict on myself when I drink. I intend to read them over and think about them regularly.

> ➢ I waste a lot of money on alcohol and then on takeaway meals such as Chinese, McDonalds, etc. because I cannot be bothered cooking when I am hung-over.
> ➢ I find it much harder to lose weight when I am drinking.
> ➢ As soon as I start drinking I sentence myself to oblivion.
> ➢ I become deceitful and lie about how much I am drinking.
> ➢ I regularly poison myself with as much alcohol as I can find.
> ➢ I go to work feeling like death warmed up and wishing that the day was over.
> ➢ I wake up in the morning wondering who I have phoned or what I had posted on Facebook.
> ➢ I put my husband through hell as he spends

evenings worrying about me.

> I encourage people I love to drink and give them the message that it is okay to drink to the alcoholic blackout stage. (This one is a strong motivator for me to stop and stay stopped.)

> I often fall asleep on the floor downstairs and eventually wake up frozen and disorientated.

> I spend the next day hating myself and am full of regret.

> My problems would not be faced because I did not have the energy to face them.

This is just a short list and not exhaustive! Even just looking at one of the above consequences of me having a drink should make any sane person stop immediately.

I love being in charge of my life and never having to deal with any of these terrible, shameful consequences of drinking again.

DAY 20

I am so grateful that I have woken up without a hangover and am ready to make the most of my day! I sound a little repetitive here but I cannot emphasis this enough.

Hallelujah - freedom!

DAY 21

I am three weeks sober today!!

This evening I am going to a retirement dinner and I am driving. I am picking up my friend who drinks most nights but does not seem to have a real problem with alcohol, although she has tried to cut down a few times and has failed. But realistically she must not be happy.

I feel totally strong and I feel stronger every day. Writing this blog is like giving myself therapy.

Tomorrow I am off to see my daughter in Newcastle. I will be up nice and early with no hangover. I will be able to make the most of the day. I feel at peace.

Happiness is seeing and acting on the obvious! Quote by me! Lol.

DAY 22

Well, my night out last night was harder than I thought. My friend has suggested that we all get together and have a little drink at her house one night. I have not told her that I have stopped drinking for good. I don't really want to tell her until I have many more days of sobriety under my belt.

You know the worst part was that I was actually considering just having a drink for a few moments. Aaaaaaaaarh. So much for my resolve!

I am not going down that road ever again. Apart from anything else I saved a fortune last night and I am feeling good this morning.

I was noticing the drinkers at my table last night and I could see that most of them were really laid back about their alcohol consumption and not that bothered about when the next round of drinks were being ordered and served. When I am drinking, my main concern is making sure that I have my fair share or even the lion's share of the alcohol on offer. When I eventually reach oblivion I have no idea how much I am consuming. Allowing my life to be controlled by alcohol in this way is a pathetic way to live.

So I am doing okay and hopefully becoming stronger and wiser with every day of sobriety.

Off on my adventure to Newcastle now!

DAY 23

I am just back from my little time away on holiday. This is the first time that I have woken up in my daughter's flat without a hangover. It felt a little strange but really good.

Life is so much easier to handle without alcohol. I am trying to be a good role model for my daughters. Having said that I must make sure that my main reason for stopping drinking is for me and not because someone else would be happy if I quit drinking. This is really important, or resentment could easily build up and a give me a 'reason' for starting again, and I definitely don't want that.

Going on holiday in a few weeks and have never been on a summer holiday before without having alcohol. It is a habit that I am determined to break. I will use the money I save on a soothing massage and some reflexology.

You need to keep strong Liz. It is worth it.

> *"One reason I don't drink is that I want to know when I am having a good time."*
>
> Nancy Astor

DAY 24

I am really tired this morning but only 9 days to work before getting 8 weeks holiday! Yes! This is going to be my first alcohol-free summer since I was probably about 15!

My body will not know what is wrong with it. Lol.

DAY 25

Life without alcohol is brilliant because I am saving a fortune! This is a prime motivator for me, so I must keep reminding myself of this fact. I am saving myself a fortune! I got one of those apps for my phone the other day called the Latte Factor. I had great fun calculating just how much I will be saving in the months and years to come. It really is incredible how quickly small amounts can add up. On the other hand I don't think I want to calculate just how much I have wasted over the years!

DAY 26

Getting better every day! I have started affirmations and because I have a tendency to give up on things, I am going to order one of those subliminal programs for my laptop. I have been hearing some great reports about these programs. My friend has lost over 30 pounds in weight and swears by them. I say nothing ventured nothing gained, or in the case of my friend, lost!

DAY 27

I have found out that my daughter is going skydiving today. Oh my goodness! I will try not to think about it. I wish I had the courage to try something daring like that! This is a danger point for me because I usually try to cover up/mask/forget my disappointment in myself with alcohol. It is a bit like trying to plaster over a crack in the wall. The only trouble is that the crack never ever gets fixed, and it just keeps showing up again. I need to be aware of this at all times.

DAY 28

My daughter loved her skydiving experience so much that she wants to train to become a skydiving instructor. Hopefully this will just be a passing phase.

I am feeling a bit bored. Monotony is setting in. My life is so boring. This is really something that I have to guard against because the next step in my thinking might be that I am missing out on something. I think that it is probably a mixture of laziness and habit. It is too easy to pick up a drink to relieve boredom.

DAY 29

I have been so bored lately and need to get my life organized to include enjoyable activities, exercise and start a new hobby. I was in bed by 9:20 last night. How boring is that?

It is the weekend and I am going off to do some retail therapy. I must find some enjoyable hobbies though. I need to find out what other people enjoy doing in their spare time. What do my friends do with their spare time? I will need to ask them. This may give me some ideas for hobbies.

DAY 30

I have been feeling really weak today. I have tried to ask myself why. What is the difference today?

I am going for a long walk. I need to get back to the place that I have been for the last month. The worst thing is that half of me is still thinking about how nice it would be to have a drink. I am going to read and think about what I have written in my blog so far.

DAY 31

I am feeling in a better place today. I have only 4 days to work then holidays! I need to stop wishing my life away and start appreciating what I do have. Today I have things in my life that at one point I could only dream about. Remember that Liz.

DAY 32

I was out with friends for a meal last night. I watched them get drunk. I talked to someone who was not drinking so it was okay. I enjoyed being able to drive home.

I woke up this morning feeling tired, because it was a late night, but thankful that I do not feel like death warmed up with a pounding hangover.

DAY 33

I must be saving a fortune between one thing and another. No expensive takeaways because I could not be bothered to cook after a night's drinking. No buying drinks for everyone when I am smashed. The list is endless. I must write this down and look back on it if I ever feel weak.

DAY 34

I was out again with friends for a meal last night. It is just typical that when I have stopped drinking that I get all of these invitations that involve alcohol!

Perhaps I should be avoiding social events that involve alcohol, but my feeling is that because I will never be able to escape people and places where alcohol is, then I really just have to get used to it.

This reminds me of the problem that ex-smokers have when they see people lighting up. My husband used to smoke 40 a day for many years but managed to stop over seven years ago now. However, if he has a whiff of tobacco smoke or sees someone smoking he will sometimes say that he could really do with a cigarette. After seven years!

I must remember that I will always be surrounded by alcohol and that I just need strategies to deal with it.

DAY 35

I am happy today because I start my holidays tomorrow! I have been invited round to my friend's house with a group of work colleagues, to celebrate the start of our holidays. I have not told them that I have stopped drinking, just that I am cutting down.

Since the long-awaited holidays have arrived, my friend has suggested that I can make an exception this time, relax and have a drink. Another friend suggested that I ask someone to drop me off and get a taxi home. Someone else said, "What a shame you are not having a drink Liz."

I am going to stick by my guns and offer to drive.

DAY 36

I am going out tonight and driving again. Nobody said anything about becoming a taxi driver when you stop drinking! I feel a sense of peace and calm though. I find it hard to really describe. I suppose that I feel a bit smug too if I am being honest. There will be thousands, hundreds of thousands even perhaps millions of people waking up tomorrow morning feeling bad because of drinking too much, and I will not be one of them for a change! I would rather be smug than hung-over!

DAY 37

It was fine last night. We all had a huge Chinese meal so the people who were drinking did not really get affected by the wine they were drinking. It is great waking up feeling good this morning!!

I am getting organized for my holiday on Thursday

today. I have 8 weeks off work so I want to make the most of it.

DAY 38

I could not sleep last night. I hate it when you lie awake like that. I do not feel too bad this morning though.

I have just realized how much I think about alcohol.

I wonder if this is normal?

I wonder if I will ever reach the stage when I never think about alcohol?

I wonder if people who have been sober for say twenty years ever feel that alcohol is not an issue and that they just do not think about it now.

DAY 39

No hangover! I really love waking up in the morning and realizing that I feel great and have the whole day ahead of me. Living with more integrity is one of the core values that I have. A life without alcohol helps me to live that value.

I am going swimming with my friend today. I know that if I make the effort to go I will end up feeling so much better. The health challenge is on.

DAY 40

No hangover, guilt or remorse. I am feeling so much better as each day passes.

LEARNING TO LIVE
YOUR LIFE
WITHOUT ALCOHOL

WHAT WILL I SAY WHEN I GO TO A PARTY OR OTHER CELEBRATION WHERE I WILL BE OFFERED A DRINK?

When I first stopped drinking, I did not feel confident telling anyone about stopping drinking. It was partly because I didn't want to admit that I had a drinking problem. After all, if I said that I no longer drank, what explanation would I give?

It might have gone something like this:

HOST: Hi Liz! Can I get you a drink? Large white wine?

ME: No thanks. I have decided to stop drinking alcohol because it has ruined my life for more years than I care to remember.

HOST: You're having a laugh!! You mean for good? I'll give you a week.

For me it was best to use the laid-back, casual approach to slowly letting my friends and family realize that I had decided to stop poisoning myself with alcohol.

Here are some "excuses": that you could use:

> I can't drink tonight because of the medicine I am taking just now.

> It's my turn to be the designated driver tonight.

> I am trying to lose weight.

> I have an early start in the morning.

WHAT WILL YOU DO WITH ALL OF YOUR FREE TIME?

There is absolutely no doubt about it: when you stop drinking, you will have so much extra time on your hands that you can use to take part in activities and hobbies that you enjoy and gain satisfaction from.

The wonderful thing is that you will now have the time - and certainly more money - to explore different hobbies or to develop interests further.

Start a hobby that you know that you might enjoy, but do not force yourself into trying one.

Here's a list of some ideas:

Aerobics
Fashion
Ornithology
Amateur Dramatics
Fencing
Painting
Antiques
Films
Angling
Photography
Paper Craft
Tropical Fishkeeping
Archery
Poker
Bridge
Polo
Fitness
Flower Arranging
Archaeology
Football
Pottery
Metal Detecting
Architecture
Aromatherapy
Postcards
Fossil Collecting
Astrology
Gardening
Psychology
Genealogy
Quilting
Badminton
Golf
Badge Collecting
Autographs
Greyhound Racing
Baking
Ballet
Reflexology
Handball
Baseball
History
Basketball
Rock Music
Beekeeping
Horse Racing
Running

Jogging
Rowing
Reading
Roller Skating
Scrabble
Hot Air Ballooning
Horse Riding
Body Building
Sailing
Breeding Animals
Sculpting
Ice Skating
Skate-
 boarding
Butterflies
Calligraphy
Sculpture
Skiing
Hot Rods
Go-Karting
Calligraphy
Skydiving
Snow-
 boarding
Jazz
Camping
Snooker
Canoeing
Jewelry
Snow Biking
Kayaking
Caravanning
Showing Dogs And
Cats
Knitting
Ceramics
Caving
Surfing
Stamp Collecting
Classic Cars
Climbing
Swimming
Chess
Squash
Lacrosse
Comics
Languages

Tennis
Computers
Magic
Ten-Pin Bowling
Mah Jong
Table Tennis
Crocheting
Theatre
Marbles
Crosswords
Croquet
Marquetry
Train Spotting
Martial Arts
Volleyball
Walking
Hiking
Rambling
Curling
Model Ships
Model Railways
War Games
Cycling
Dancing
Monopoly
Web Design
Weather Forecasting
Digital Art
Motorbikes
Wind Surfing
Dominoes
Wall Art
Drawing
Weaving
Keyboard
Piano
Guitar
Saxophone
Drums
Embroidery
Origami
Yoga
Pilates
Zumba

The list is endless, and the secret is to give a few of these a try, no matter how random you think they are. You never know; you might just end up with an absorbing hobby that will give you the opportunity to make friends who do not drink. Sometimes people who have stopped drinking can feel isolated because their social lives are built around drinking and people who drink.

This might be a time to think about your friends who frequently drink. Do you think that they are truly happy? Are they healthy looking? Have they achieved their potential in life and at work? Have they confided in you that they feel that they are drinking too much and that they are spiraling out of control?

You might also consider using the money and time that you are saving to start your own online or offline business. There is a whole world of opportunity available to you.

When I felt myself getting weaker and wanting to have a drink, I would make myself **remember** what it was like to wake up with a hangover, feeling mentally and physically bad. I really used my imagination to get back to the place that I had been desperate to escape from. I made myself feel the hangover - the dry mouth, the pounding head, wanting to stay in bed until I felt better, etc.

I also imagined the regret I would feel and think about who I would have upset with my drinking.

You see, when you stop drinking, it is too easy to remember what you think you're missing and talk yourself into a drink.

KEEPING YOURSELF STRONG

Here is a list of things that I read over to remind myself of where I have been and where I do not want to go back to. This helped me to stay strong after I had made the decision to stop drinking.

- ➢ Sitting on a doorstep peeing yourself.
- ➢ Not remembering a thing.
- ➢ One is too many, and a thousand is not enough.
- ➢ Vodka and orange.
- ➢ Making sure that I have more than anyone else.
- ➢ Graduation parties.
- ➢ Drinking my husband's lager.
- ➢ Missing work.
- ➢ Texting people.
- ➢ A million horrible hangovers.
- ➢ Getting fatter and fatter.
- ➢ Palpitations.
- ➢ Drinking more and more.

> ➤ Christmas.
> ➤ Driving to my friends.
> ➤ Feeling ill and tired all of the time.
> ➤ Skinny dipping and losing my clothes.
> ➤ Being refused entry to a pub.
> ➤ Gran Canaria lunch.
> ➤ Arguing with the girls.
> ➤ Mary's fire in back garden.
> ➤ Never being able to control it.
> ➤ Sending my husband out for more.
> ➤ Spending a fortune.
> ➤ Eating rubbish the next day.
> ➤ Wasting days of my life feeling lousy and waiting for the day to end.
> ➤ Hating myself for ruining my life.
> ➤ Falling outside our local pub.
> ➤ All-day migraines.
> ➤ Drinking parties that nearly went too far!
> ➤ Blackpool with Mary.
> ➤ Sitting like a fat blob with a drink in my hand.
> ➤ Feeling trapped and helpless to stop the madness.
> ➤ Being depressed.
> ➤ Edinburgh!!
> ➤ College cheese and wine.
> ➤ Wishing my life away.
> ➤ Going on Facebook and abusing people or

finding "friends."

➢ Being boring.

➢ Waiting for people to finish their drink so another round can be ordered.

➢ Being overweight, bloated, and sluggish most of my life!!!!!!

➢ Feeling like s**t.

A constant battle - pathetic. I am never going back there ever again because it is a dark hole of DEGRADATION.

I suggest that you make your own list and refer to it when you need to. Go through each reason, thought, or event and really think about it; experience it again in your mind. Use this technique to remind yourself of why you made the decision to stop drinking in the first place.

> *"To get what you want,*
> *STOP doing what isn't working."*
>
> Dennis Weaver

Use everything in your power to help you escape.

SUMMARY

REASONS FOR STOPPING DRINKING

You will get back your self-respect and feel proud of yourself again.

You will not have that nagging guilt dragging you down.

You will be mentally present for your friends and family at all times.

You will be able to lose weight (if you need to) because you will not be taking in empty alcohol calories, and you will never feel the need to feed a hangover again.

You will save a fortune.

As alcohol is a depressant and a toxin, so you will feel much happier and healthier when you have removed it from your system.

You will have lots of spare time to fill with satisfying holidays and activities.

You will be able to organize your life better.

You will be a great role model for your children and people that you care about. Your family and friends will be able to stop worrying about you and what you might do to yourself when drunk.

You will be present for people and will not be stuck in an alcoholic fog where you become lost in your own little world.

You will probably live a longer, healthier life.

You will have much more energy and feel brighter.

You will get more of the things that you really want to do accomplished and you will produce better work of a higher standard.

You will not be spending the rest of your life trying to work where your next drink will be coming from.

People will comment on how much healthier you look.

You will be able to cope so much better and will not turn molehills into mountains nearly as much.

Your liver and other vital organs that have been affected by alcohol consumption will have a chance to heal.

You will have less chance of developing dementia, osteoporosis, and other horrible illnesses later in life.

You will be able to make better plans for your life and carry them through.

I know from bitter experience just how difficult it can be to finally make the decision to say enough is enough and mean it. The secret is getting your mindset right. You need to stop drinking for yourself first and foremost.

Stopping drinking needs to be seen as a time for joy and happiness and not for mourning the loss an old friend. If alcohol were a real person, he would be one of those people that you cross the street in order to avoid talking to. If anyone has caused you real pain and harm in your life, then you would want nothing to do with that person, right? You need to keep telling yourself that the transitory, illusionary pleasure that you receive from alcohol is **not worth the price that you have to pay!**

Are you worried about a relation or a friend drinking too much as well? The best way to help them is to show them, with your actions, how great life can be without alcohol. If you want to change others, you need to set the example. If they see you enjoying your life without alcohol, then you will have gone a long way to helping set them free.

A WORD ABOUT RELAPSE

Please remember that if you fall off the wagon and have a drink, it is not the end of the world. Many people make several attempts before they finally get it! I certainly did. As Les Brown says, **"It is not over until you win."** Each day without alcohol is a victory - a victory to be enjoyed and savored. Keep going and do not give up because the rewards are amazing and empowering.

The fact that you have become aware of your problem and are taking steps to defeat it means that you will never go back to wanting to settle for your alcohol-soaked life again. You will have tasted the joy and freedom that stopping abusing alcohol brings, and even if you pick up the glass or the bottle again, you will find yourself yearning to get that peace of mind and freedom back.

Remember you are giving nothing up and at the same time gaining your life and self-respect back.

MY LIFE TODAY

Every day I am sober, I am getting stronger and stronger. You will get stronger too.

A simple statement here will suffice.

Since I have stopped abusing my mind, body, and soul with alcohol, I have never been happier!

I enjoy my life. I am true to my authentic self. I live up to my personal values and beliefs every day. I am not only having a positive impact on myself but also on my family and friends. I am a good role model for my children. Yes, I still have days when things are not so good, but I know that these days would be considerably worse if I were still drinking. I AM FREE!

You can be free too! I wish you every success.

Remember you have nothing to lose and everything to gain!

All the best,

Liz Hemingway

If this book has helped you, I would be grateful if you could write a review for it so that this message of hope can reach other people who are suffering at the hands of alcohol. Thank you.

Amazon.com - http://amzn.to/16TIi30

Amazon.co.uk - http://amzn.to/16vHBk4

STOP DRINKING
START LIVING!

In this book Liz Hemingway continues to provide motivation, insight and hope for anyone who feels that alcohol is causing them problems in life.

Liz explains the different stages that she went through in order to reach a better, happier life without the need for alcohol. She describes various, common scenarios that may have you running back to the bottle if you are not careful. Problem drinkers have to get real with themselves and wake up to the fact that they have the power to change their lives and never look back.

This book looks at the different aspects and stages that problem drinkers go through. First of all it will help you to work out whether or not you have a problem with alcohol.

It then considers the possibility of moderating your drinking.

It supports you in your decision to stop drinking by

giving you strategies and tips that Liz uses to maintain her sobriety in a world that is full of drinkers. The book is uplifting, positive, and full of hope and inspiration. It also includes some real life stories of men and women who have been affected by alcohol but have managed to find a better, much happier way to live.

A word from the author, Liz Hemingway

> "Men and women, from all over the world, are suffering right now. Their lives are being made miserable and often intolerable by alcohol. It is a silent epidemic happening in homes near you. Perhaps it is affecting you or someone that you love.

> I was a victim.

> I was quietly being torn apart by alcohol. It crept up on me slowly but surely. I have learned to stand up to this bully and say enough is enough. I have finally woken up to a few basic truths that helped me escape from my nightmare.

> I decided that I wanted the real me back who was happy, healthy and true to my values. I asked myself this question

> If I loved myself truly, deeply and properly would I really allow myself to experience this pain and misery?

> I started treating myself as someone I did truly and deeply love and began showing this in my thoughts, actions and choices. I have expanded

on these thoughts, actions and choices in my new book entitled *Stop Drinking Start Living!* I finally reached the point where I knew that I could not go on hurting myself with alcohol any longer and did something about it. If you can relate to any of this then you will find my book *Stop Drinking, Start Living!* will empower you to love and care for yourself better. In doing so it will help you to see alcohol in its true light, make you stronger, reclaim the real you and get rid of the hangovers, pain and regrets forever!'

Find *Stop Drinking Start Living!* on Amazon today.

Amazon.com: http://amzn.to/1c74VqM

Amazon.co.uk: http://amzn.to/19Wcda1

ABOUT THE AUTHOR

Liz Hemingway writes from the heart and with brutal honesty. She has experienced first-hand the devastation that alcohol can cause. It takes over your mind and soul and takes everything it can from you, including your self-respect.

Liz shares her escape from alcohol plan that worked for her in the hope that it will help you to live the life that you always wanted for yourself and for the people that you love.

She wants everyone who is being torn apart by alcohol to know that it is possible to finally escape from it and experience joy, freedom, and happiness for themselves.

INDEX

18803102R00068

Made in the USA
San Bernardino, CA
29 January 2015